Jason Gruhl & Ignasi Font

EVERYTHING IS CONNECTED

DEDICATION

TO THE MOUSE
AND THE MOUNTAIN,
THE FLOWERS AND
STARS...
AND TO YOU AND ME.

AND TO EVERYONE QUIET
ENOUGH TO SEE
THEY'RE THE
SAME.

bala kids

An imprint of Shambhala Publications, Inc.
4720 Walnut Street
Boulder, Colorado 80301
www.shambhala.com

9 8 7 6 5 4 3 2

Printed in China

♾ This edition is printed on acid-free paper that meets the American National Standards Institute Z39.48 Standard.
♻ Shambhala Publications makes every effort to print on recycled paper. For more information please visit www.shambhala.com.

Bala Kids is distributed worldwide by Penguin Random House, Inc., and its subsidiaries.

Library of Congress Cataloging-in-Publication Data
Names: Gruhl, Jason, author. | Font, Ignasi, illustrator.
Title: Everything is connected / Jason Gruhl; illustrated by Ignasi Font.
Description: First edition. | Boulder: Bala Kids, 2019. | Summary:
Highlights the many ways we are all linked to the world around us.
Identifiers: LCCN 2018019443 | ISBN 9781611806311 (hardcover: alk. paper)
Subjects: | CYAC: Stories in rhyme.
Classification: LCC PZ8.3.G933 Ev 2019 | DDC [E]—dc23
LC record available at https://lccn.loc.gov/2018019443

EVERYTHING iS CONNECTED.

AND SiNCE *YOU* ARE PART OF EVERYTHING, YOU ARE *CONNECTED* TO EVERYTHING.

TO MOMS AND TO DADS,
TO SISTERS AND BROTHERS,
UNCLES AND COUSINS,
GRANDFATHERS, GRANDMOTHERS.

YOU'RE CONNECTED TO FRIENDS AND TO TEACHERS AT SCHOOL,

AND EVEN TO PEOPLE YOU *DON'T THINK ARE COOL.*

AND THEY ARE CONNECTED TO YOU.

YOU ARE ALSO
CONNECTED TO HEDGEHOGS

...and CATS and DOGS and SQUIRRELS and BIRDS,
RABBITS and COWS and
DEER by the HERDS,

MONKEYS, TARANTULAS,
DOLPHINS and SNAKES...

FRIEND, YOU'RE CONNECTED TO EVERY

BIG SMALL HAIRY SLIMY SNUGGLY SCALY FLOPPY FLAPPY BRISTLY BUZZY BEAUTIFUL

CREATURE ON EARTH...

EVEN BLOBFISH.

"BLOBFISH?!" YOU SAY.
"SURELY NOT THAT! THEY DON'T LOOK LIKE ME, TALK LIKE ME, OR ACT LIKE ME...

AND THEY PROBABLY STINK!"

BUT, YOU SEE, WE'RE CONNECTED.
WE ALL PLAY A PART.

IN LIFE WE'RE THE SAME,
WE'RE ALL BLOBFISH AT HEART!

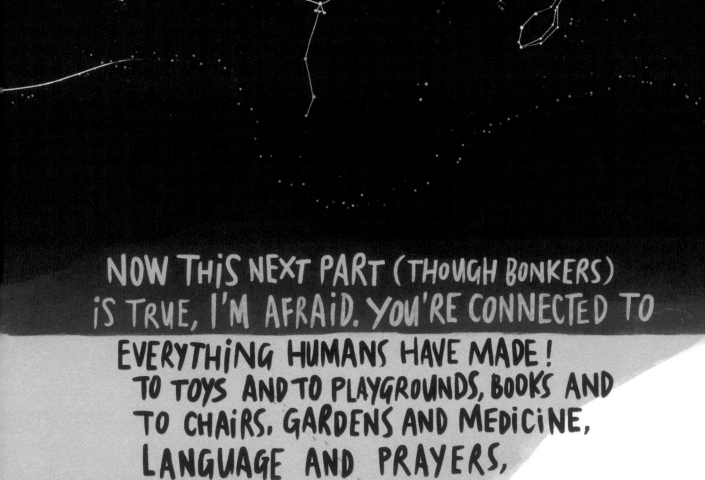

NOW THIS NEXT PART (THOUGH BONKERS)
IS TRUE, I'M AFRAID. YOU'RE CONNECTED TO
EVERYTHING HUMANS HAVE MADE!
TO TOYS AND TO PLAYGROUNDS, BOOKS AND
TO CHAIRS. GARDENS AND MEDICINE,
LANGUAGE AND PRAYERS,

BUILDINGS AND BICYCLES, BUSES,
BALLOONS, HAMMERS AND PAINTBRUSHES,
TRACTORS AND SPOONS.

BUT ALSO TO
CHICKEN POX, BULLIES
and LIES, TO GREED
and
POLLUTION and TRASH
PILED HIGH.

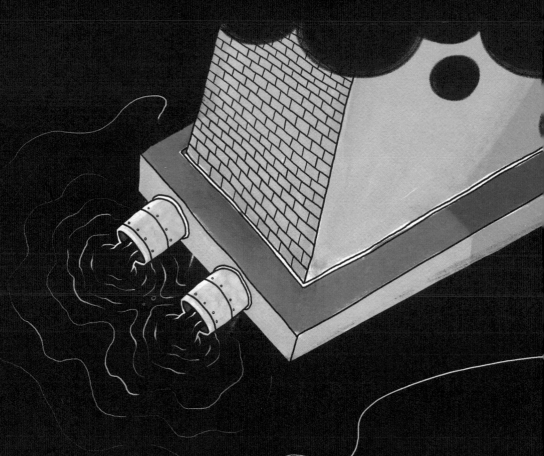

YOU'RE NOT JUST CONNECTED
TO THINGS THAT YOU LIKE —
THINGS THAT ARE COMFORTABLE,
EASY, OR NICE. AS A HUMAN,
YOU'RE PART OF THE EVERYTHING-NESS.
AND SOMETIMES IT'S SCARY
AND A BIG UGLY MESS!

BUT THE GOOD NEWS, MY DEAR,
IS THAT YOU ARE QUITE
POWERFUL, A FORCE THAT'S
IN EVERYTHING—

TO HYDROGEN, NITROGEN, NANOBOTS TOO.
YOU'RE CONNECTED TO THEM.
THEY'RE CONNECTED TO YOU.

TO SPACESHIPS AND ALIENS
WITH NOSES LIKE HOSES!

YOU'RE CONNECTED TO ALL THAT WILL BE OR HAS BEEN.

YOU'RE *THIS VERY MOMENT,* WHERE ALL THINGS BEGIN.

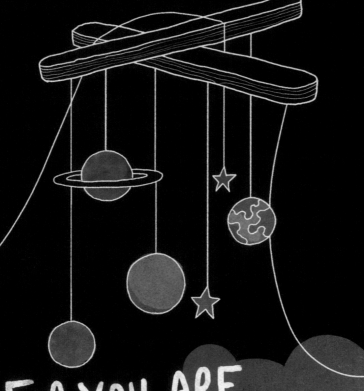

FOR YOU ARE
THE SUN
AND THE MOON
AND THE STARS.

VENUS AND JUPITER,
NEPTUNE AND MARS,

COMETS AND GALAXIES,
VOIDS AND BLACK HOLES.

YOU ARE THE UNIVERSE,

PERFECT and WHOLE.

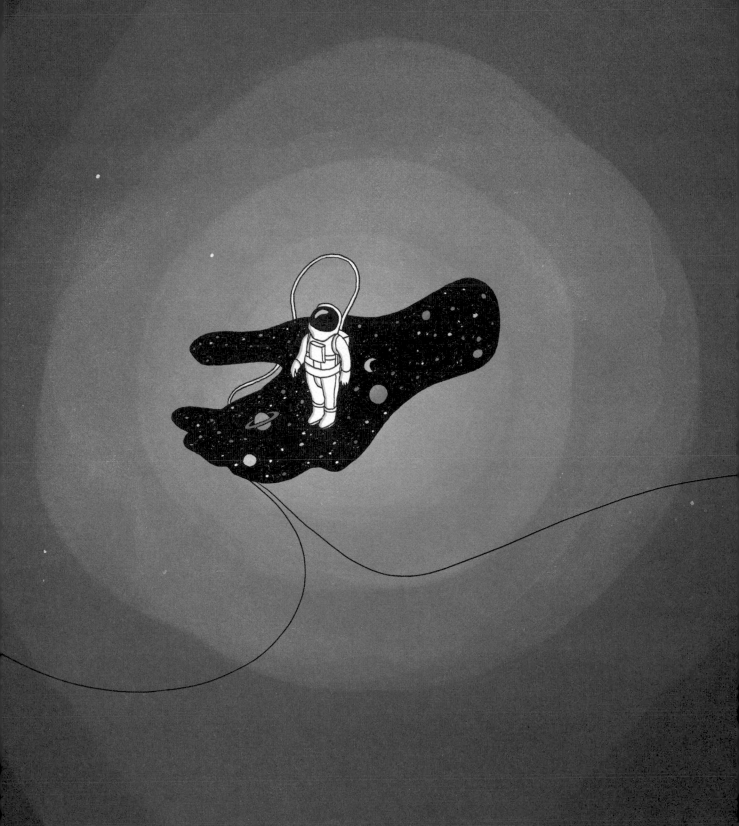

AUTHOR'S NOTE

WHY SHOULD WE CARE ABOUT A CHILD IN PAKISTAN, THE CORAL REEFS IN AUSTRALIA, OR A COW IN CHINA? THESE SORTS OF QUESTIONS CAME UP MANY TIMES FOR MY STUDENTS DURING THE TWENTY YEARS I SPENT IN EDUCATION. WE SOMETIMES HAVE A HARD TIME SEEING HOW THE LIVES OF OTHERS OR WHAT'S HAPPENING ON THE OTHER SIDE OF THE WORLD IMPACTS US. BUT WHEN WE REALLY LOOK, WE SEE THAT EVERYTHING IS CONNECTED.

THIS BOOK DOESN'T TELL YOU HOW THINGS ARE CONNECTED, AND THAT WAS AN INTENTIONAL CHOICE. I BELIEVE IT IS UP TO EACH READER TO FIGURE THE "HOW" OUT FOR HIMSELF OR HERSELF, AND EVEN TO QUESTION IT! WHILE WE MAY NOT ALWAYS WANT TO BE CONNECTED TO EVERYTHING, THERE IS A DEEP REASSURANCE IN REALIZING THAT WE ARE—THERE'S A LITTLE BIT OF "YOU" IN EVERYTHING. AND BECAUSE OF THAT, YOU ARE NEVER, *NEVER* ALONE. SO, GET ON OUT THERE AND SEE FOR YOURSELF. BE BRAVE. THERE'S A BLOBFISH SOMEWHERE THAT WILL THANK YOU.

ACKNOWLEDGMENTS

JASON

TO JONATHAN, WHO BELIEVES I CAN
DO ANYTHING.

TO WILLOW, WHO SHINES AND SHARES
WHEREVER SHE GOES.

TO MAKENNA AND MIKAELA,
FOR YOUR FIRST IMPRESSIONS.

AND TO IGNASI,
FOR YOUR FRIENDSHIP
AND FOR SAYING YES.

IGNASI

TO LINUS.

TO LU, THE MOST BEAUTIFUL LIGHT
I'VE EVER SEEN.

TO MY MOM, FOR HER INFINITE SUPPORT.

TO MARTA, FOR HER SMILE.

AND TO JASON.
THANKS FOR SHOWING UP ON THE WAY.

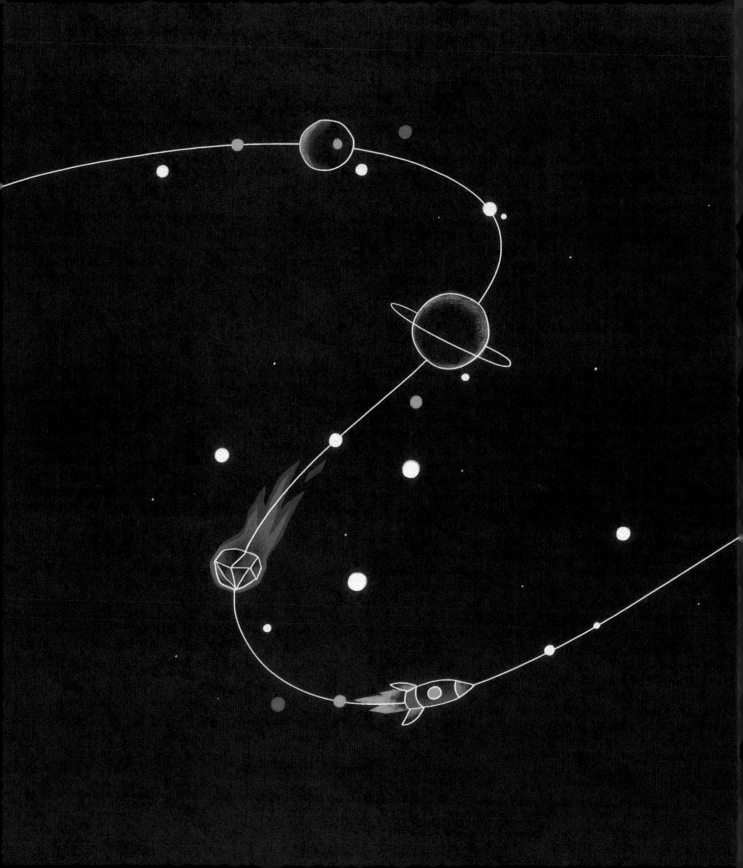